Rocky Mountain
National Park

by Mike Graf

Reading Consultant:
Dr. Robert Miller
Professor of Special Education
Minnesota State University, Mankato

Bridgestone Books
an imprint of Capstone Press
Mankato, Minnesota

Bridgestone Books are published by Capstone Press
151 Good Counsel Drive, P.O. Box 669, Mankato, Minnesota 56002
http://www.capstone-press.com

Library of Congress Cataloging-in-Publication Data
Graf, Mike.
   Rocky Mountain National Park / by Mike Graf.
   v. cm.—(National parks)
   Contents: Rocky Mountain National Park—How the Rockies formed—People in the
Rockies—Animals—Plants—Weather—Activities—Safety—Park Issues—Map activity—
About national parks—Words to know—Read more—Useful addresses—Internet sites—
Index.
   ISBN 0-7368-1378-0 (hardcover)
   1. Rocky Mountain National Park (Colo.)—Juvenile literature. [1. Rocky Mountain
National Park (Colo.) 2. National parks and reserves.] I. Title. II. National parks
(Mankato, Minn.)
F782.R59 G73 2003
917.88'69—dc21   2001008095

Editorial Credits
Blake A. Hoena, editor; Karen Risch, product planning editor; Linda Clavel, designer;
   Anne McMullen, illustrator; Alta Schaffer, photo researcher

Photo Credits
Digital Vision, 1
James P. Rowan, cover, 10
Jon Gnass/Gnass Photo Images, 14
Kent & Donna Dannen, 6, 8, 12, 16, 17, 18
Tom Till, 4

1 2 3 4 5 6 07 06 05 04 03 02

Table of Contents

Colorado

Rocky Mountain National Park

The Rocky Mountains lie in the western United States, Canada, and Mexico. They form the largest mountain chain in North America. In 1915, the U.S. government set aside part of the Rockies as a national park.

The government creates national parks to protect unique natural areas such as the Rockies. People cannot build or hunt on park lands. But they can camp, hike, and view the wildlife and scenery in the park.

Rocky Mountain National Park is in northern Colorado. It covers more than 400 square miles (1,040 square kilometers) of land. More than 3 million people visit this park each year.

Rocky Mountain National Park is the highest park in the United States. More than 100 mountain peaks in the park are higher than 10,000 feet (3,000 meters) above sea level. One-third of the park also is above the tree line.

Sprague Lake is in Rocky Mountain National Park.

How the Rockies Formed

Millions of years ago, the western area of the United States was actually a sea. Over time, sand and clay filled in the sea. This soil mixed with lava from nearby volcanoes and hardened into rock. The rock at the bottom of the mixture became granite. The base of many mountains in the Rocky Mountains is made of this hard rock.

Plates make up Earth's crust. These large sheets of rock float over pools of magma, or melted rock. When plates meet or rub against each other, they create great amounts of pressure. This force helped form the Rockies. When the plates below the granite met, the pressure pushed up the earth and rock to form mountains.

Glaciers shaped the Rockies. These slow-moving sheets of ice carved out the mountains' features. They made ridges, deep valleys, and canyons. They also created moraines. These piles of earth and rock form natural dams that create mountain lakes.

Andrews Glacier is one of the glaciers that still exists in the Rocky Mountains.

People in the Rockies

American Indians have traveled in the Rockies for thousands of years. Ute Indians hunted elk and moose in the mountains during the summer. Their spear points have been found throughout Rocky Mountain National Park.

In the 1800s, miners, trappers, and explorers began to travel to the area. Explorer Stephen H. Long recorded the location of Longs Peak in 1820. It is the highest peak in the park at 14,255 feet (4,345 meters) above sea level. In 1868, an explorer named John Wesley Powell climbed to the top of Longs Peak. In 1873, Anna Dickenson became the first woman to climb to the top of Longs Peak.

In the late 1800s, Enos Mills ran Longs Peak Inn. Tourists stayed at this hotel when they visited the area. Mills talked to people all over the United States about the beauty of the Rocky Mountains. His talks helped convince lawmakers to set aside part of the Rockies as a national park.

Enos Mills often photographed the features in the Rockies. He is called the "Father of Rocky Mountain National Park."

Animals

Rocky Mountain National Park is a popular place to view wildlife. Large animals such as bighorn sheep, moose, elk, and mule deer roam throughout the park. A few black bears and mountain lions also live in the Rockies.

Many smaller animals live in the park. Squirrel-like marmots live high in the mountains. Coyotes can be heard barking at night. Visitors may see beavers in mountain ponds and streams.

Several types of birds nest in the park. Peregrine falcons, prairie falcons, golden eagles, and red-tailed hawks fly throughout the area. They nest in trees or on cliffs. Ptarmigans are a type of grouse. These birds live on the ground in grassy areas of the park. Ptarmigans' feathers turn from brown to white in the winter. The color change makes them difficult for predators to see. Predators are animals that hunt other animals for food.

Yellow-bellied marmots live in Rocky Mountain National Park.

Plants

Thick forests grow in the lower areas of the park. These forests include quaking aspen, ponderosa pine, and Colorado blue spruce trees. Lodgepole pines also grow in the park. American Indians used these tall, straight trees to build their homes.

Subalpine forests of Douglas fir, subalpine fir, and Englemann spruce trees grow in the mountains. These forests grow just below the tree line in mountainous and northern areas.

Elfin forests grow near the tree line. These forests consist of short trees. Strong winds, cold temperatures, and lack of water keeps the trees from growing tall. Groups of trees often grow behind rocks, where they are protected from the wind.

The tree line begins at 11,500 feet (3,500 meters). At this height, it is difficult for trees to grow because of the harsh weather. Mosses, lichens, and wildflowers such as orchids and columbines grow above the tree line.

Trees do not grow above the tree line in the mountains.

Weather

The weather at Rocky Mountain National Park can change quickly. Sudden afternoon thunderstorms often occur. High in the mountains, snow can fall any time of year.

In spring, the weather varies. One day can be calm and sunny. The next day might be cold and snowy. Snowstorms may last for several days.

Summer days begin sunny. But in the afternoon, clouds build up around mountain peaks. Thunderstorms occur at this time of day.

Fall mornings are chilly. But the temperatures warm up in the afternoon. Park visitors can see the leaves of trees such as aspens turn color in early fall.

Winters in the Rocky Mountains are cold and harsh. The weather is very windy in the mountains. Blizzards and snowstorms often occur. Up to 30 feet (9 meters) of snow may fall during the winter. Some of the park's roads are closed during this time.

The leaves of trees such as aspens turn color during fall in the Rockies.

Activities

Many people come to Rocky Mountain National Park to hike, camp, and view wildlife. The park has more than 300 miles (480 kilometers) of trails. People can hike to see mountain streams, lakes, and waterfalls. One trail even leads to an old mining town, Lulu City. Fishing and bird watching also are popular park activities.

Many people come to the park to mountain climb. Some visitors hike on trails to mountain peaks, like Longs Peak Trail. Others rock climb the park's steep cliffs. In winter, some visitors ice climb up frozen waterfalls.

Safety

Safety is important in the Rockies. The mountains' steep slopes and cliffs can be dangerous for hikers. People should be careful near snow-covered and ice-covered ledges. These areas can be slippery. Wet rocks near waterfalls also can be slippery.

Even on warm, sunny days, people should be prepared for cold weather. Park visitors should bring warm clothing with them on hikes. The weather can change quickly in the mountains. Snow can fall any time of year.

Park Issues

Rocky Mountain National Park is facing several issues. One problem is visitors feeding park animals. When small animals or birds eat natural food, they get water from the food. But they do not get enough water from human food. Human food also has too much salt. Salt causes the animals to become dehydrated. Park workers are teaching visitors why feeding animals is harmful.

Another problem is the large number of park visitors. These people create a great deal of trash and pollution. Park visitors should clean up any garbage that they create. They should carry out everything that they bring into the park.

Park visitors should try not to harm the natural conditions of the park. Visitors can do this by hiking on existing trails. They also should avoid approaching animals or damaging plant life. These actions will allow everyone to enjoy the park's beauty.

Park rangers teach visitors about Rocky Mountain National Park.

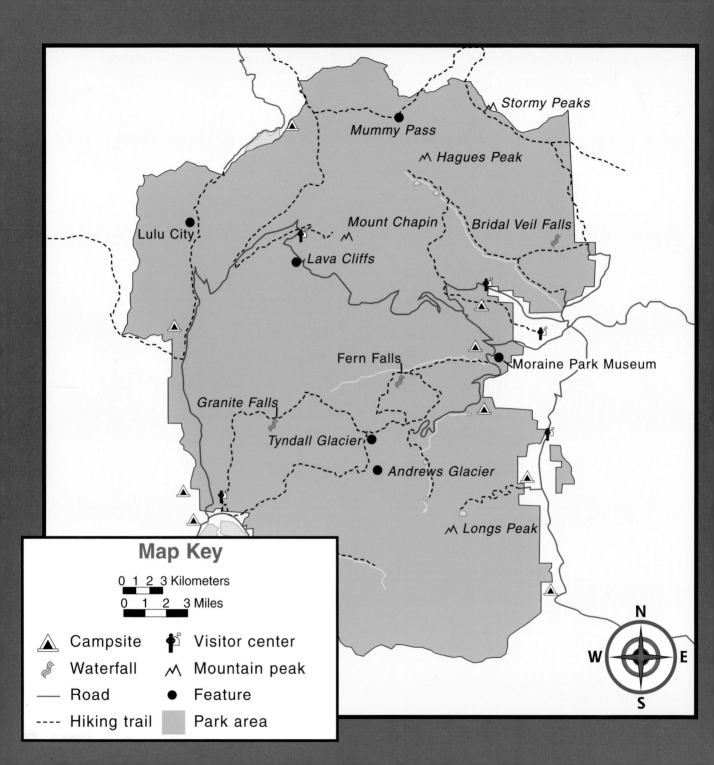

Stormy Peaks

Mummy Pass

ʌ Hagues Peak

Mount Chapin

Bridal Veil Falls

Lulu City

ʌ

Lava Cliffs

Fern Falls

Moraine Park Museum

Granite Falls

Tyndall Glacier

Andrews Glacier

ʌ Longs Peak

Map Key

0 1 2 3 Kilometers

0 1 2 3 Miles

△ Campsite

🚶 Visitor center

𝄃 Waterfall

ʌ Mountain peak

— Road

● Feature

---- Hiking trail

Park area

N
W   E
S

Map Activity

The shortest distance between two places is a straight line. But Rocky Mountain National Park has many canyons and mountains. Hiking through steep canyons and over tall mountains is not easy or safe. Park visitors should follow park trails and roads as they hike. See how mountain features change the distance you travel between two places.

What You Need
Ruler
20-inch (51-centimeter) piece of string

What You Do
1. Find a campsite on the map. Then pick a place to visit. This site can be a mountain peak or another site.
2. Using the ruler, measure the distance between your campsite and the site you picked to visit. Use the map's scale to find how far this distance is in miles (kilometers).
3. Next, measure the distance you have to travel. Place one end of the string on your campsite. Then lay the string down, following trails and roads, until you reach the site. Measure the length of string with the ruler and use the scale to find the distance in miles (kilometers). How great is the difference between the two distances?

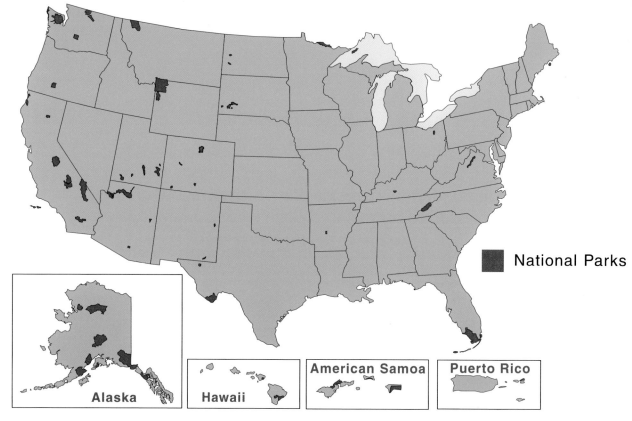

National Parks

About National Parks

In 1916, the U.S. government formed the National Park Service. This organization was created to oversee all U.S. park lands. The National Park Service runs nearly 400 areas. These sites include recreational areas, natural landmarks, and historic sites such as battlefields. The National Park Service also oversees more than 50 national parks. These parks protect unique natural areas such as the Rocky Mountains.

Words to Know

dehydrated (dee-HYE-dray-tid)—not having enough water
glacier (GLAY-shur)—a slow-moving sheet of ice found in mountains and polar regions
harsh (HARSH)—unpleasant or hard
plates (PLAYTSS)—the sheets of rock that make up Earth's outer crust
precipitation (pri-sip-i-TAY-shuhn)—the rain and snow an area receives
sea level (SEE LEV-uhl)—the average surface level of the world's oceans
subalpine (sub-AL-pine)—consisting of plant life that lives just below the tree line in mountainous and northern areas
tree line (TREE LINE)—the point on a mountain where trees can no longer grow because of weather conditions
unique (yoo-NEEK)—one of a kind

Read More

Bograd, Larry. *The Rocky Mountains.* Ecosystems of North America. New York: Benchmark Books, 2000.
Petersen, David. *National Parks.* A True Book. New York: Children's Press, 2001.
Raatma, Lucia. *Our National Parks.* Let's See. Minneapolis: Compass Point Books, 2002.

Useful Addresses

National Park Service
1849 C Street NW
Washington, DC 20240

Rocky Mountain National
  Park
1000 Highway 36
Estes Park, CO 80517-8397

Internet Sites

National Park Service—Rocky Mountain National Park
http://www.nps.gov/romo
U.S. National Parks Net—Rocky Mountain National Park
http://www.rocky.mountain.national-park.com

Index